365 Days of Real Talk:
Wordplay to Get You Through Each Day

Keshia Bates

365 Days of Real Talk:
Wordplay to Get You Through Each Day
Copyright © 2021 Keshia Bates
ISBN: 978-1-7358344-7-4

All Rights Reserved. No part of this publication may be reproduced, distributed or transmitted in any form or by any means, including photocopying, recording, or other electronic or mechanical methods, without the prior written permission of the publisher, except certain other noncommercial uses permitted by copyright law. All quotes and scriptures are cited within the content, reference by the author, or are unknown and are not being credited to the work of any contributing author of this book.

Cover by Design Place
Published by One2Mpower Publishing LLC

Introduction

"365 Days of Real Talk: Wordplay to Get You Through Each Day" is a compilation of daily quotes and affirmations. These are not the quotes that you may be used to reading, but straight forward wordplay that is nothing short of "Real Talk". These quotes are a lighthearted, witty approach to days that may be challenging, are eye opening, and even days when we need a little boost. An important reminder thought is that every day is a BLESSING!

"365 Days of Real Talk: Wordplay to Get You Through Each Day" was inspired by conversations, personal struggles and real-life issues that affect us all. Subject matters that will resonate with all readers, regardless of status or background. No matter what our differences may be, we can all connect through real situations, real struggles and definitely through "REAL TALK."

Keshia Bates

DAY 1

Don't pay attention to what people think of you, unless they are thinking about helping you pay some bills. If they aren't PUTTING IN… Tell them to hold their TWO CENTS.

Day 2

Beware of people: there are "reporters" and "repairers". Some just want something to TELL and others really want you to do WELL!

Day 3

You don't have to think you're BETTER than ANYONE to want BETTER for YOURSELF!

Day 4

It's best to SHAKE some people when you're on the MOVE.

Keshia Bates

Day 5
How you treat people here is how He'll GREET you up there!

Day 6

Your POSITION won't help you when you TRANSITION! BE careful who you look down on.

Day 7

Pay attention to the ones that can no longer HIDE it anymore. Their intentions were always in plain sight!

Day 8

Imagine me having YOUR back and you having MINE. You're PUSHING me and I'm PULLING you along, you're UPLIFTING me, and I'll never let you FALL.

Day 9
Instead of DIGGING ditches and DROPPING negativity, try PLANTING some seeds. The HARVEST will be much greater.

Day 10

We all COMMIT and don't ADMIT! Be grateful that our SINS don't determine our WINS.

Day 11
We can do BETTER if we do it TOGETHER.

Day 12

It will be easier for all people to STICK together, once we realize that the enemy is trying to STICK to us ALL.

Day 13

Why is skin color so DISPLEASING when we should all be PLEADING… the BLOOD?

Day 14

There'll never be a RIGHT time when we're already having a HARD time, but always make TIME, even in TOUGH times because you don't know how much time you actually have.

Day 15
People that have some things MISSING will always be the ones MESSING!

Day 16

Don't let BROKEN people keep you from getting your FIX. You have too many blessings waiting on you.

Day 17
The devil can't DRAIN what you don't ENTERTAIN!

Day 18
You may think you don't have anything WORTHY of ENVY, but PEACE is something many people can't AFFORD!

Day 19

If they're always in the LOBBY, it may be that they're afraid of HEIGHTS! Some people are content with just "talking". Others want to see what's at the TOP.

Day 20
Let people THINK what they want to THINK. Situations usually turn out better than they THOUGHT!

Keshia Bates

Day 21
Remember there's nothing to PROVE when God has already CONFIRMED.

Day 22
They have no choice but to SWERVE when they realize who you SERVE. #Covered

Day 23
Always REMEMBER the ones that never FORGET about you.

Day 24
If the goal is to EAT, then STARVING for attention definitely won't get you FULL.

Day 25

Things won't always be the BEST< but fully understand that they could always be WORSE.

Day 26
Without TESTS, you wouldn't know to stay PREPARED. Always PRAY so you can PASS.

Day 27
Don't TRIP when they set you up to FALL, you'll always STUMBLE upon a blessing.

Day 28

We let each other down when we just LOOK to see, instead of LOOKING OUT to see if we can help.

Day 29

If you want to keep GETTING, you have to learn to FORGIVE! That doesn't mean that you have to FOOL with them, it means you're no longer a FOOL for them.

Day 30
If you put all of your effort into RUNNING your household, you won't have time to try to RUIN anyone else's.

Day 31

What they do as SHADE to you, God uses as a COVERING for you! Thank HIM for protection.

Day 32

SANITIZING your house is not as effective as DISINFECTING your temple! Get rid of the hatred in your HEART!

Keshia Bates

Day 33
Despite it ALL, it's in God's hands.

Day 34
Don't live life in FEAR but be cautious to FOOLISHNESS.

Keshia Bates

Day 35
You don't know everyone's STORY, yet we all share the same author.

Day 36

We always notice that LIFE is SHORT, but we haven't realized how LONG it takes us to get it together.

Day 37
Try to make it RIGHT, you don't know much of it you have LEFT.

Day 38
The world needs HEALING. We are "sick" in more ways than just one!

Day 39
Focus on the BLESSINGS and not the BATTLES.

Day 40

Don't roll so "HOLY" and still land in HELL! You can't COUNT theirs and not MEASURE your own. He hates the sin, but still loves the sinner.

Keshia Bates

Day 41
When we LOSE faith, the enemy FINDS a way in.

Day 42
No matter where you're sitting, you'll never SIT HIGH ENOUGH!

Day 43
Stop JUDGING others, we're all GUILTY of something.

Day 44
You shouldn't worry about who SUPPORTS you when you know who SUPPLIES you.

Day 45
There's a thin line between LOVE and FAKE. Always recognize the difference between someone who's LOYAL and a SNAKE.

Day 46

The only time some people come TOGETHER is to be AGAINST other people. Don't be the one to cause DRAMA. The story doesn't always END WELL.

Day 47
They may try to get in your business, but don't let them in your SPIRIT!

Day 48

To reduce your stress level: Stop worrying about people more than they're worried about themselves! They need to want it more than you want it for them.

Day 49

Don't put God in it when you need to look GOOD! He sees when you cut up too! Be real with YOURSELF. He already knows the real you!

Day 50

Never forget that it could be YOU! Stop putting your MOUTH on situations where you should be using your HEART.

Keshia Bates

Day 51
Always PRAY and never PREY.

Day 52
You don't have to run with "Who's who" to know that you're somebody.

Day 53
When you learn to STAND ALONE, it teaches you to STAND STRONG.

Day 54
They may not SEE to it that you get there, but GOD will let them WATCH you arrive.

Day 55
Never count it as a LOSS, always count it as a LESSON!

Day 56

In order to CLEAN UP (your life), you must first take out the TRASH. Delete it. Disconnect from it. Dismiss it. Destroy it. If you kick it to the CURB, you won't have to worry about unnecessary baggage.

Day 57
Stop giving people the BENEFIT of the doubt when they are only BENEFITTING from you! Don't make excuses if people are USERS.

Day 58

Some people get a little bit, then they FORGET! You can have it today and it can be gone tomorrow.

Day 59
Don't let COMING UP be your DOWNFALL.

Day 60
Don't DOWNPLAY someone else's blessings because you haven't UPGRADED your prayer life.

Day 61

Everybody can talk a "good game" from the SIDELINES but can't perform when the COACH finally puts them in. Never let other people call the PLAYS in your life.

Day 62

Sometimes things TURN AROUND when people TURN on you! The DOOR they walked out of was the one GOD was waiting to OPEN.

Day 63
Do more handling business than minding other people's business.

Day 64

You don't have to live a PERFECT LIFE. Just pray for PERFECT PEACE.

Day 65

When folks do you wrong, He'll surely make it alright! Always be grateful and not hateful.

Day 66

You say "next year" will be your year AGAIN. Don't wait because time sure doesn't.

Day 67
Stop PROCRASTINATING and start PRODUCING.

Day 68
Everybody that's in your EAR ain't coming from the HEART! Some are just a DETOUR to distract you from the right DIRECTION.

Day 69

When you USE people, make sure you keep up with the RECEIPT! The EXCHANGE won't be worth what you get in RETURN.

Day 70
Don't allow bitterness to EAT you up, it keeps you from living life to the FULLest!

Day 71

Always PUSH others, but don't let them make you fall! It's okay to HELP people as long as it doesn't HURT you in the process.

Day 72
Sometimes SABOTAGE comes in CAMOFLAUGE. Don't trust every SMILE and don't hold too tight on every hug!

Day 73

Just because you have a BACKGROUND doesn't mean GOD won't put you out FRONT! You can't QUALIFY for the job if you don't have EXPERIENCE.

Day 74

No matter who STOPS along the way, don't let anything STOP you from moving on! You're UNSTOPPABLE!

Day 75
Don't let things linger beyond its PURPOSE in your life.

Day 76
If there's NO POINT, then what's the POINT! POINT. BLANK. PERIOD!

Day 77
You will never GAIN if you like to see others LOSE!

Day 78
Don't let people with NOTHING cost you EVERYTHING.

Day 79

The only reason some of us are still STANDING is because GOD is still KEEPING us.

Day 80
We're all a MESS, yet HE continues to BLESS.

Day 81
If your "friends" can't push you OVER THE TOP, don't let them push you OVER THE EDGE!

Day 82
Some people want to see you FLY, while others want to see you JUMP! Choose your friends wisely.

Day 83
It's best to follow ACTIONS and not ACTING! It's what you DO and not what you SAY.

Day 84

God may have u on the WAITING LIST now, but the blessing will be more than you can handle! Keep HOLDING ON! #KeepStriving

Day 85

Don't waste time FIGHTING people that are BATTLING with themselves! They're MAD at life, so why let them UPSET yours?

Day 86

I'll SHARE with you, but I won't let you STEAL what's mine! JOY shouldn't cause JEALOUSY. Just find you some, it's FREE!

Day 87

The devil doesn't KNOW love. That's why when you SHOW love, He reveals Himself.

Day 88

Stop ANSWERING people that only ASK you to do things for them! It's okay to REFUSE when they never RECIPROCATE.

Day 89
Don't let anyone else RUIN what you're BUILDING.

Day 90
Anything you won't MISS should be quickly DISMISSED.

Day 91
Stop letting people SPILL their drama into your life. It always gets MESSY!

Day 92
Pillow talk should never make it to the SIDEWALK! The LESS they know, the more BLESSINGS flow.

Day 93

You're too OLD to wonder why people don't LIKE you and they're too OLD to not LIKE themselves! They only TALK about you because what they're doing ain't worth HEARING.

Day 94
Never trust people that know the "DIRT" on everybody. They're dirty themselves.

Day 95
Never be ashamed of your PAIN, but always have FAITH in the PROMISE.

Day 96

Be careful how you FALL OUT with people. You may have to LEAN back on them to PICK YOU UP.

Day 97
When you're not SEEKING approval, things start to look a whole lot better!

Day 98
Stop SEARCHING where there is NO RESCUE. They can't SAVE you!

Day 99
Instead of watching SHAPES, start paying attention to PATTERNS! Just because it's SHINING doesn't necessarily mean it's bright.

Day 100

Don't be surprised at what level people will STOOP to when they're already LOW! Always RISE above what's beneath you.

Keshia Bates

Day 101
Don't let DIVISION be the reason that things don't ADD UP!

Day 102

They'll SPREAD what you DID before they SHARE what you're DOING! Don't let the CHATTER matter.

Day 103

Don't focus on the LIES. Keep your eyes on the PRIZE! Their STORIES don't measure up to the GLORY.

Day 104

You never GET AWAY with it, He just lets us GET BY. It if wasn't for GRACE, some of us couldn't show our FACE.

Day 105
Let no one STRESS you to DEPRESS you. Let them GO so that you can GROW.

Day 106

Try to remain CIVIL even when you know they aren't RIGHT! What they're GIVING won't stand a chance to what they'll GET! Vengeance is the Lord's!

Day 107
Don't always be part of the MIX. The wrong INGREDIENTS can change the FLAVOR!

Day 108

We are all capable of getting into some "stuff", and even though HE allows us to STEP in it, He doesn't make us STAY in it.

Day 109
You don't have to pay attention to the SIGNS. There's something out there that will STOP you! When God speaks, it's wise to LISTEN.

Day 110
Be careful with your words! It's hard to RETRACT when you OVERREACT.

Day 111

Stop seeking REVENGE and be SATISFIED with REVELATION! Everything is CLEAR when you SEE who you're dealing with.

Day 112
When you try to do HALF way right, God will make sure you're FULLY covered.

Day 113
Stop doing folks WRONG and continue expecting things to turn out RIGHT.

Day 114
Some people will never give others CREDIT, those are the people that always get DECLINED.

Day 115

None of THEIR business should be any of YOUR business when you are minding YOUR OWN BUSINESS.

Day 116

Don't worry when people start TRIPPING on you. Every hole they DIG, they end up FALLING IN!

Day 117
You don't have to try EVERYTHING to know that some things don't amount to ANYTHING!

Day 118
People do WHAT they want, WHEN they want, and for WHO they want to do it for!

Keshia Bates

Day 119
Stop being RIDE or DIE for relationships that are already DEAD.

Day 120
Stop doing what's "HOT" before you get BURNED! What everyone else is doing ain't for EVERYBODY.

Keshia Bates

Day 121
They might KNOCK it, but they can't BLOCK IT.

Day 122

It's okay for people to CHANGE. Just don't allow them to keep SWITCHING UP on you!

Day 123
Don't want SOMETHING so bad that you'd do ANYTHING for it! You may GO DOWN trying to COME UP.

Day 124

Don't PRETEND like you've got it. Just ACT like it's on the way! Lookin' good ain't better than livin' good!

Day 125
Stop STICKING BY people that STEP OVER you!

Day 126
In order for CONFIRMATIONS to CONTINUE you must be CONSISTENT!

Day 127
RESERVE your energy, some HOOKUPS can cause you to DISCONNECT.

Day 128

They may say it as a JOKE, but please take it SERIOUSLY! Always LISTEN for the LESSON.

Day 129

Stop making EXCUSES for people that don't make EFFORT! If they never SHOW YOU, stop SHOWING UP.

Day 130
You can't be PETTY and PRODUCTIVE, get it TOGETHER instead of TEARING people apart.

Keshia Bates

Day 131
Waiting your turn doesn't mean rush through everyone else's. Celebrate others!

Day 132

When you are the BIGGER person, you always receive BIGGER blessings.

Day 133
People can't GET OVER on you when you're already COVERED.

Day 134
When God says "NO", it doesn't mean "never", it means not right now! Wait on Him.

Day 135
CHALLENGES come…. We can either RUN or GET IT DONE!

Day 136

Most people that RUN their mouths don't actually RUN anything! Work more so you're worth more.

Day 137
Try not to go BACK and FORTH, you can't MOVE FORWARD

Day 138
Be BETTER than the BITTER! You can't pass the TEST if you're focused on the MESS.

Day 139
Don't let the FIRST person you call when you NEED something be the LAST person you call when you HAVE something.

Day 140

Life is 3 categories: BUSINESS, BASICS, and BOGUS
BUSINESS is what pays you.
BASICS are what you pay.
BOGUS is what PLAYS you.
#StayFocused

Day 141

Life will never be STRESS FREE but try your best to be SUCKER FREE! Their mission is to SUCK the life out of you!

Day 142
Don't be so quick to put your STAMP on their issues and never ADDRESS what's going on with yours.

Day 143

Don't BASE your decisions on people that have no FOUNDATION! Waiting to see "WHAT THEY'RE GOING TO DO" is the reason why you never GET ANYTHING DONE.

Day 144
Whatever you use to FUEL yourself, make sure it's not that E&J-ENVY and JEALOUSY. It takes you down like no other.

Day 145

Just because you REMOVE people out of your PICTURE doesn't mean it won't still DEVELOP! Sometimes they're blocking the LIGHT.

Day 146

You may not have all the FINER THINGS, but EVERYTHING is gonna be JUST FINE.

Day 147
What you've DONE can't compare to what GOD CAN DO! He'll take you from ASHAMED to ACCLAIMED.

Day 148
They want you to STOP so they won't have to try to KEEP UP!

Day 149
If your day is spent talking about people, chances are you're not MAKING MONEY and that makes absolutely NO SENSE!

Day 150
The PROBLEM with people is that we quickly SEE other people's problem but are BLIND to our own.

Day 151

We all have been CAUGHT UP. We just haven't been CAUGHT YET. It's called grace and mercy.

Day 152
Demons TRAVEL and uninvited guests take longer to LEAVE.

Day 153
All ATTENTION ain't good ATTENTION! Being THIRSTY only makes you look WATERED DOWN.

Day 154
It doesn't take a CLIQUE for you to try to FIT. Stick with the FEW that will always remain TRUE.

Keshia Bates

Day 155

When you know they have potential to STING, you shouldn't hang around certain BEES.

Day 156

They may wonder how you can HANDLE it all, but it's only because of who's HOLDING you up! Keep on keepin' on.

Keshia Bates

Day 157
When people are "not speaking" to each other, most times it's because neither is willing to LISTEN! Make it RIGHT and forget who's WRONG!

Day 158
A HARD pill to swallow can become a DOSE of reality!

Day 159

Be careful how you view other people's situations.
If you get ALL INTO YOURS, it will definitely keep you OUT OF THEIRS!
Be so FOCUSED until it makes you FORGET what anyone else is doing.

Day 160

Comparison is the THIEF of joy. Don't get ROBBED while searching for your Joy! You don't need to "BE LIKE" anyone other than who you are and should already LOVE.

Day 161
Don't allow SCARED people to put FEAR in you! You can do ALL things.

Day 162

The BODY style won't matter if the MOTOR is in bad shape. Its what's on the inside that matters.

Day 163

Too many people PRETEND they never do any WRONG, for FAKE people that are never going to do RIGHT.

Day 164

Never judge a SITUATION where you have no PARTICIPATION! Don't say what someone should DO because that someone could quickly become YOU.

Day 165

You had to go through that situation to prepare for your transformation! God is about to do a NEW thing.

Day 166
Stop letting people "JOYRIDE" that aren't bringing you any JOY.

Day 167
They may not SEE to you getting there, but GOD will let them WATCH you get it DONE.

Day 168
Get with people that want to build BUSINESS! BOND over BLESSINGS, not mess and stressing.

Day 169

Some people can't find any GOOD in anything if things aren't going GOOD for them… Try to Find something GOOD in everything!

Day 170
Life's problems aren't meant to DROWN you, they help you SAVE someone else.

Day 171
They can't tell you how to GET somewhere they've never been! All they can do is COMPARE and TALK.

Day 172
We all have done things we're not PROUD of. That doesn't make us any less worthy of HIS Promises.

Day 173

Try not to put yourself in a PREDICAMENT with people that are PREDICTABLE! You know how it's gonna TURN OUT, so don't keep TURNING to them.

Day 174
PRAY and STAY OUT OF THE WAY!

Day 175

If you FEEL like people are always targeting you then it's time to FALL on your knees! Sometimes we fail to SEE because we won't LOOK at ourselves! It can't be EVERYBODY.

Day 176

Never let other people's OPINION be an OPTION!

You can't PREVENT the enemies' plan, but you can be PREPARED! Stay PRAYED UP!

Day 177
Every time you COMPLAIN, you give the devil authority to DRAIN! It's not as bad as it could be.

Day 178
You can't focus on the RAIN if you're soaking in the SON!

Day 179
Don't use your EX as an EXCUSE for you not to be a better EXAMPLE.

Day 180
If you don't FIX your heart, you're gonna stay BROKEN.

Day 181

You'll never go anywhere holding on to hurt! HURT will never HELP YOU.

Day 182

Some people are FOR whoever's in their FACE, keep those people out of your SPACE!

Day 183

It's best to keep your lips SEALED if you don't want it SPILLED! Move in silence.

Day 184

You don't have to be living your "BEST LIFE", but always do the BEST YOU CAN!

Keshia Bates

Day 185
When the devil sees that you're HALFWAY HAPPY, he becomes a FULL TIME HATER!

Day 186
You don't have to live a PERFECT LIFE, just pray for PERFECT PEACE.

Day 187

There are people that wish they were able to TALK to their family members, yet there are others that won't even SPEAK to theirs. Family matters!

Day 188

Sometimes not MENDING fences can TEAR the whole house APART! PATCH things that are able to be FIXED while you still can.

Day 189

A GOOD woman brings out the BEST in a man! A MOTIVATING ENCOURAGER can definitely replace a NAGGING WORRIER. Be his peace.

Day 190

With the way they TALK about their "FRIENDS", you should be glad they aren't one of yours! The COST of being a FRIEND doesn't include SELLING OUT in the END.

Day 191
God has the power to OUTLAST ALL OF THESE OUTLAWS.

Day 192
If they can't respect your GROWTH, it's because they haven't MATURED.

Day 193
You don't have to know people to PRAY for them! Their today can be your TOMORROW.

Day 194
They LOVE to see you GOING THROUGH but HATE to see you GET THROUGH!

Day 195
If they LIE and tell you they wouldn't do it if they were you, the TRUTH is they WANT to and CAN'T.

Day 196
Pay attention to the ones that don't like it when you get ATTENTION.

Day 197
Even when it's not the OUTCOME you were hoping for, don't let it change the OUTLOOK that you're praying for.

Day 198

People don't know how to TAKE you when they're so used to TAKING ADVANTAGE! Continue to do things because of your HEART and let God handle theirs.

Keshia Bates

Day 199
People afraid of CHANGE are the ones that'll SWITCH up on you when you make a change for the better.

Day 200

Let no one PUSH you to the point where they PULL you from the people that matter most.

Day 201
They may say "SOMEBODY SAID...", but please believe it's everything THEY WANNA SAY.

Day 202

Respect the fact that a coward respects you! They don't have the COURAGE to CONFRONT a CONQUEROR.

Day 203

If you see that they can't keep it together, don't let them make you lose all you got! You know better.

Day 204

These days you can't KILL people with KINDESS. You gotta CONQUER them with CONFIDENCE!

Day 205
Don't allow people to TEAR down what they didn't help to BUILD.

Day 206

There's a difference between those who NEED to know and people who just WANNA know! Those that NEED to know want to HELP, and those that want to know NEED help.

Keshia Bates

Day 207
The only reason some of us are STILL STANDING is because God is STILL KEEPING us!

Day 208
It can be difficult to MOVE UP in life if you're afraid to MOVE ON! Gotta keep the faith.

Day 209

Sometimes you need to take these "JOKERS" seriously! If they said it on the SLY, they're probably hatin' on the HIGH. Pay attention.

Day 210

Stop looking for REPLACEMENTS when God will always REPLENISH! Anything that LEAVES was never meant to STAY.

Day 211

If it hasn't happened YET, it's not YOUR TIME! Don't miss your blessing trying to SPEED UP someone else's. It's coming.

Day 212
When you stop trying to PLEASE others, you'll finally have the PLEASURE of living.

Keshia Bates

Day 213
People will see a PROBLEM when you make PLANS towards PROGRESS.

Day 214
Don't waste time FIGHTING people that are BATTLING with themselves! They're MAD at life, so why let them UPSET yours?

Day 215
You don't have to be SEEN for them to know you're THERE!

Day 216

Watch ACTIONS not ACTIVITY. It's not what they SAY, it's what they SHOW.

Keshia Bates

Day 217
We have done everything under the SUN, but it's nothing like a covering from the SON.

Day 218
Sometimes SABOTAGE wears CAMOUFLAGE! Don't mistake an ENEMY for an ALLY.

Day 219

Be GRATEFUL not GREEDY! If you can't appreciate the LITTLE THINGS, you won't be able to handle the BIG things.

Day 220

If you keep listening to the people in the STREETS, you'll find yourself OUTDOORS! Do what WORKS for the people that are WORKING with you.

Keshia Bates

Day 221
People who ALWAYS want something for NOTHING usually end up with NOTHING. Now ain't that something?

Day 222
There are some DISTURBED people that live to DISTURB others! Your PEACE bothers people. Protect it!

Day 223

At some point, you have to see that some things are POINTLESS! Do what you can, pray about what you can't!

Day 224
Stop dealing with MESS that won't ever PROGESS! This includes people, places, and things.

Day 225
Don't allow MATERIAL things to shape the FABRIC of your life!

Day 226

Don't miss your HELP because you're too stuck on your HURT.

Keshia Bates

Day 227
Don't HEAR what they say, but WATCH what they do! You'll SEE!

Day 228
EMPTY people can't FILL big shoes!
It's FREE to talk, but it COSTS to walk.

Keshia Bates

Day 229
Do it where it COUNTS, not to keep up with WHO'S COUNTING.

Day 230
You can't solve their PROBLEMS without creating some ISSUES for yourself!

Day 231
It's not WISE to make enemies but be SMART enough to know that everyone is not a friend.

Day 232
Don't allow people who don't contribute to the roof OVER YOUR HEAD to hold things OVER YOUR HEAD.

Keshia Bates

Day 233
Even if no one ever CHEERS you on, remember that doesn't stop your chances of WINNING!

Day 234
Stop worrying about what "they said" if it ain't making no BREAD!

Day 235

Stop FRONTING for folks that won't have your BACK!

It's TIME OUT for putting things off because you don't have that much TIME! Get THINGS DONE.

Day 236
Do the work, work on you, and let the work speak for itself!

Keshia Bates

Day 237
CUT some people off, not because they did anything to you, but because they just aren't doing it for you!

Day 238
Don't WASTE TIME with a WASTE of TIME.

Day 239

The people that can't STAND you may be the same ones that SIT at your table! Don't BREAK BREAD with people that want to see you STARVE.

Day 240
Never listen to people that always have something to SAY but are never SAYING ANYTHING! They're CALCULATING, but it doesn't ADD UP!

Day 241
Don't be so quick to expose their DIRTY laundry if you haven't checked yours for HOLES!

Day 242
No matter what anyone else brings to the TABLE, always be able to FEED YOURSELF.

Keshia Bates

Day 245
Follow your DREAMS, they will lead you to your DESTINY.

Day 246

People will think you've LOST your MIND when you finally FIND some sense! As long as they're able to do you WRONG, it's ALRIGHT.

Keshia Bates

Day 247
It shouldn't take for someone to DIE for us to decide we need to LIVE!

Day 248

WATCH as well as PRAY for those WATCHING and PREYING! They SEE you, but they can't STOP you!

Day 249

Leave people ALONE that aren't BOTHERING you! Find something constructive to do.

Day 250
When you carry excess BAGGAGE, you're either gonna be running LATE or you'll always MISS your destination.

Keshia Bates

Day 251
HOLDING ON to things can HOLD you down.

Day 252

We never GET AWAY with it. He just lets us GET BY! If it weren't for GRACE, some of us couldn't show our FACE!

Keshia Bates

Day 253
You can't RIDE with everybody! They'll eventually THROW you under the BUS!

Day 254
Don't feel the need to COMPLAIN or EXPLAIN to people that don't PROVIDE.

Day 255

Everyone has done SOMETHING in their PAST, but don't let THAT stop you from doing ANYTHING with your FUTURE.

Day 256

The same ones that EGG you on can't wait to see you with EGG on your face! They're waiting for you to CRACK under pressure. #StayFocused

Day 257
If your JOB is to be in other folks' business, find something else to OCCUPY your time. Be a VOLUNTEER.

Day 258

If you never THOUGHT they would, you better THINK AGAIN! People tend to TURN on you with no SIGNAL! Always use caution.

Day 259

Stop being an "AMEN" friend and start being a TRUE friend. If they can't tell you the WHOLE truth, then the friendship is a WHOLE lie!

Day 260

Don't listen to the gossip of what "SOMEBODY SAID" if they couldn't say it to you! You can CUT the drama if you CUT OFF the source.

Day 261

Stop trying to figure out what you DID to people, especially the ones that haven't DONE anything for you! Let them stay MAD. You'll probably have a lot more PEACE.

Day 262

Be glad that the PREYERS don't stop your PRAYERS from getting through!

Keshia Bates

Day 263
Every time you think it LOOKS BAD, just LOOK BACK at everything He's already brought you through.

Day 264

A HOUSE is just a MORTGAGE. A CAR is just a NOTE. Don't envy a person's lifestyle unless you're willing to COPY their work ethic!

Day 265

At every new LEVEL be prepared to encounter a new DEVIL! He comes to attack when you're on a good track.

Day 266

Even though people have the strength to throw DIRT on your name, they still don't have the POWER to bury you.

Day 267
The best way to battle is on your knees! Let God fight your battles.

Day 268
Don't waste energy trying to PROVE that you're a GOOD person to people that have the WORST intentions for you.

Day 269

Forget who's always ready to RIDE when the gas tank is FULL and pay attention to the ones WILLING TO PUSH when you're EMPTY.

Day 270

People that live to COMPETE will always lose SLEEP! Confidence in SELF makes you COMPETE with no one else!

Keshia Bates

Day 271
Don't let what other people have GOING ON affect where you're GOING.

Day 272

People that like to see you doing WORSE than them are the people you should to stay away from! They are NO GOOD.

Day 273

No one is really concerned with how things are GOING until they think you're GOING THROUGH it. Keep pressing forward.

Day 274
A new mindset will show you what is PETTY and what is a PRIORITY.

Day 275

You can't change anyone else's MIND, but you can CONDITION your own.

Day 276
You can't play DIRTY and expect the STAINS not to show! Your day will come.

Day 277

Don't be boosted by what you want to hear. It's what you need to hear that will send you SOARING.

Day 278
Never judge people for what they do. PRAY for them like somebody prayed for you!

Day 279
Ignorant people won't show COURTESY but expect God to keep showing them MERCY! Love thy neighbor.

Day 280

If you truly did it from your heart, don't look for Praise! The reward is much greater later.

Day 281

If you're WORRIED about people being WORRIED about you, then it's obvious that you need something ELSE to do! What you're doing should have you too occupied to care!

Day 282
God wouldn't give you a VISION that He can't bring into FRUITION! Plan the work and Work the Plan.

Keshia Bates

Day 283
Don't let BACKWARDS thinking be the reason you're BEHIND! Leave the PAST so u can Leap into the FUTURE.

Day 284

God isn't SKIPPING over you. He's waiting for you to JUMP IN! You gotta work if you wanna EAT!

Day 285

Always forgive the people that do you WRONG. Then, let them figure out why they can't get anything right!

Day 286

Stop going OUT OF YOUR WAY for people that are just IN THE WAY! They may be the HOLD UP interfering with your COME UP!

Day 287

People will SPEND time and energy trying to FIGURE a way to SUBTRACT something from you that they didn't ADD! If GOD made a way for you to have it, He'll make an even better way for you to keep it!

Day 288
Stay TUNED in to the Lord and you'll never miss a BEAT. While keeping everything and everyone TOGETHER, don't let you be the one who's falling apart!

Day 289

You have a "friend" as long as you have an OPEN HAND! Start saying "NO" and watch how fast they'll GO.

Day 290

The ones you think you can't LIVE without are the main ones sucking the LIFE out of you! Anything you weren't born with, learn to live without!

Keshia Bates

Day 291
When two-faced people DOUBLECROSS you more than ONCE, they're really not to blame! They don't know who they are either!

Day 292

It's not wise to SIT with people if you know they can't STAND you! A smiling face doesn't always represent a warm embrace.

Day 293
Two-faced people MASTERMIND being FAKE but forget that they FAIL the Master for real!

Day 294
Instead of COMPLAINING, we need to get in COMPLIANCE! We overlook signs but won't search OURSELVES.

Day 295

Before you go rattling BONES in someone else's closet, make sure the BODIES that are in yours are under control.

Day 296

Everyone has a DARK part of their past that should make them want to work HARDER for a BRIGHTER future.

Day 297

Better SAFE than SORRY, but it's SAFE to say some are just SORRY! They won't take themselves to WORK and try to take what others WORK FOR!

Day 298
They always PAY ATTENTION to everything when they never get RECOGNIZED for ANYTHING!

Day 299

You can take a RISK with an enemy, at least they know their place, but none are more DANGEROUS than the ones that smile in your FACE!

Day 300
Every relationship has PROBLEMS, it's best to handle them in PRIVATE!

Day 301

They wait on you to TALK ABOUT IT then they go TALK ABOUT YOU! You can't VENT to people that have no FILTER.

Day 302

"Cheer on" the love, life, and success of others. It's only practice for you to "SHOUT" when it's your turn.

Keshia Bates

Day 303
There's enough for EVERYBODY! He never runs out of blessings.

Day 304
If you don't PLAY into the SAME folks DRAMA, it ends up being a whole DIFFERENT story!

Day 305

You may miss the FINISH line if you wait for everyone else to START! Don't get SIDETRACKED in someone else's LANE.

Day 306

Do all you possibly can when you know people that are DOWN, because you most DEFINITELY will not always be up!

Day 307

Some things you let go on TOO LONG, with people you should've let go of LONG ago.

Day 308
Anything you won't miss should quickly be DISMISSED.

Day 309
Why BRAG when we're all filthy RAGS! Don't talk it more than you walk it!

Day 310
If you can't BACK it up, it's BEST just to SHUT it up!

Day 311

If you TALK down, ACT down, and LOOK down, then how do you expect to COME UP? If your GROUP Is not moving, then it's time to REGROUP.

Day 312

How much PAIN do people have to cause to realize they're the one that's HURTING! Hurt people hurt people.

Day 312
If people TELL you what you can't do, just keep SHOWING them that God can!

Day 313
Make BELIEVERS out of UNDER ACHIEVERS!

Day 314
Some people STOOP so low and are still unable to STAND up against you.

Day 315
Respect your past, but don't allow it to disrespect your future!

Day 316

Don't let the MISTAKE cause you to doubt your FAITH! No matter the circumstances, He still gives so many chances.

Day 317
Don't look at the PRETTY PICTURE and forget that it took time to DEVELOP.

Day 318

To keep your (relation)SHIPS afloat, keep other people out the BOAT! You work hard ROWING, and they do overtime THROWING.

Day 319
The CIRCUMSTANCES we go through only strengthen us for the CHALLENGES we grow through.

Day 320

You can't force people to strive for more and seek NEW LEVELS, but what you don't have to do is STOOP to theirs.

Day 321

FORGIVE who hurt your feelings but never FORGET how they made you feel!

Day 322

Always be eager to learn. The more knowledge you acquire the more you're able to inspire!

Day 323

You can't be UNDERHANDED and EXPECT to come out on TOP! People that are always getting OVER are the ones barely getting by!

Day 324

Often times, you have a better BOND with people with those you share no BLOOD! Some people can be so 100 that it makes you forget all the ZEROS.

Day 325
Looking for attention will always lead to the WRONG kind. If they can't see how great you are, then maybe you should keep seeking.

Day 326

Don't force yourself into something that you'll eventually have to wiggle your way out of.
It doesn't matter if people know your name, make sure GOD knows your HEART.

Day 327
People only watch you SHOW, but GOD is watching for the GROWTH.

Day 328
Don't dwell on your PAST when God gave you a PASS.

Day 329

People will certainly WALK AWAY, but God will show you why they couldn't STAY.

Day 330
The devil can always LEAD you to do WRONG, but he won't ever GUIDE you to do RIGHT.

Day 331
Don't LOSE yourself trying to prove that you're WINNING.

Keshia Bates

Day 332
Happy can't be bought, but LOVE can be taught.

Day 333
Trying to keep up with "their" house will leave you in the Po' House or with No House at all!

Keshia Bates

Day 334
Living above your MEANS is not the MEANING of LIVING. Always strive for more, but always ACT your WAGE.

Day 335

Watch your "NEW FRIENDS" that love you not but couldn't stand you back then. They have a MOTIVE!

Day 336

People will COMMENT about you but will never COMMEND you! So, don't expect them to be happy for you when they aren't happy with themselves.

Day 337
Part of some people's TENSION is caused by a third-party seeking attention.

Day 338
FORGET who lost you being FOOLISH and remember who keeps you in your FOOLISHNESS.

Day 339

You can never prepare for PAIN, but what you can do is pray for PEACE. You never know the LOSS other people have taken, so try not to ADD to it.

Keshia Bates

Day 340
Don't see WHO or WHAT'S in the WAY. Look at the fact that HE keeps making a way!

Day 341
Don't BRAKE for ROADBLOCKS, just GO AROUND.

Day 342

It's not who has the MOST, it's who makes the MOST out of what they have.

Day 343

Nothing BELONGS to you. We're all on BORROWED time, so be sure to GIVE it your ALL.

Day 344
Most people that want to see you UNHAPPY can't stand to look at themselves.

Day 345

The only way for people not to PUSH YOUR BUTTONS, is if you stop giving them POWER and disconnect the service.

Day 346

You can't prevent the enemies' plans, but you can be PREPARED. Stay PRAYED UP! There is POWER in your PRAISE.

Day 347
Everything you ACKNOWLEDGE does not require a RESPONSE! Sometimes the best comeback is not getting back at all.

Keshia Bates

Day 348
It's impossible to be allergic to hard work and expect SUCCESS to taste sweet!

Day 349
A few COINS shouldn't CHANGE how you PAY attention to people! Don't get so uppity that it makes you look DOWN on others.

Day 350

If you go PEEPING in your neighbor's WINDOW, be mindful that you left your FRONT DOOR OPEN!

Day 351
When you're so busy in other people's business, you don't even realize that you're neglecting your own.

Day 352

Don't be so eager to report the TEA. You may be BREAKING NEWS with the coffee in the morning.

Day 353
LOYALTY is not who STANDS by you in good times. It's who STICKS with you in the bad.

Day 354

CHERISH the people that SEE you through, not the ones that are just SEE THROUGH! Don't confuse friendship with fellowship, one is temporary.

Day 355
Stop PATCHING UP things that can't be FIXED! Let it GO before it takes you AWAY!

Day 356
Don't let people use you as a REST AREA when you should have let them EXIT.

Day 357
They may ADD a bunch of LIES, but they can't take AWAY the FACTS! The truth can stand alone.

Keshia Bates

Day 358
If you find out folks like to cause you MISERY, it's best to make them part of your HISTORY!

Day 359

Stop SEARCHING for what you WANT and watch you FIND what you NEED! It doesn't always look like what you're LOOKING FOR.

Keshia Bates

Day 360
Always FOLLOW your first mind, it is usually the best LEADER!

Day 361

STAND tall and WALK on your own before you allow them to RUN it in the ground. It's not about the OLD you, it's about the BOLD you!

Keshia Bates

Day 362
The people that you put on a FRONT for probably need BACKUP too! LIVE for you and not for others' view!

Day 363

Having FAKE people around you is like buying KNOCK-OFF goods. No matter how badly you wanna believe they're REAL, deep down inside, you know they won't ever be!

Day 364

Before you make your health and weight loss goals for the New Year, be sure to drop the dead weight! It's the EASIEST to lose because it's the HEAVIEST!

Day 365

As long as they INQUIRE, God will keep taking you HIGHER! They can keep being NOSY, He'll keep it in their FACE.

Keshia Bates

www.ingramcontent.com/pod-product-compliance
Lightning Source LLC
Chambersburg PA
CBHW060453090426
42735CB00011B/1973